PASSPORT TO FLAVOR

QUICK & EASY INTERNATIONAL RECIPES

Del Monte *Quality*

Passport To Flavor

Join us in a delightful culinary adventure around the world, sampling delicious international cuisines. Enjoy a visit to the bistros of France for a bowl of Tomato French Onion Soup. Explore the hills of Italy with outstanding pastas and pizzas. Sample some of the exotic foods served in such faraway places as Thailand, Morocco and China. Take an exciting trip across the United States to discover the tasty treats of American regional cooking, including Sausage Ham Jambalaya from Cajun country, Manhattan Turkey à la King, the Midwest's Heartland Shepherd's Pie and Santa Fe Corn Bake.

Del Monte makes it easy to bring the great flavors of the world home to your kitchen with our unique line of tomato products. Each product is designed to make cooking at home easy and delicious. We offer a creative way to season dishes with an authentic international or American regional twist. Pre-cut and pre-seasoned, Del Monte Stewed Tomatoes provide the busy consumer with great taste, convenience and value.

Each recipe includes Prep and Cook times to show just how quickly you can get it on the table. Most of these great-tasting recipes call for 8 ingredients or less—what could be easier?

Watch for the low fat and low fat/low salt color bars next to recipe titles. These recipes have 30% or less of the calories coming from fat, less than 300 mg of sodium per serving. They also include calories, fat, cholesterol and sodium counts per serving.

There are also dishes especially suited for parents and kids to make and eat together. What kid can resist Cheeseburger Macaroni, Sloppy Dogs or Taco Pizza? These easy-to-make recipes are a wonderful way for families to have fun together in the kitchen. Look for the blue diamond symbol following these recipes.

Whether you're looking for a super-quick idea for busy weeknight dinners or fabulous meals with a foreign flair, you'll find the perfect recipes right here in your *Passport to Flavor*.

3

Italian Delights

*Pastas, pizzas and more—
nobody will be able to
resist these incredible
Italian meals!*

CHUNKY PASTA SAUCE WITH MEAT

8 ounces linguine or spaghetti
6 ounces ground beef
6 ounces mild or hot Italian sausage links, sliced
½ medium onion, coarsely chopped
1 clove garlic, minced
2 cans (14½ ounces *each*) DEL MONTE® Pasta Style Chunky
   Tomatoes
1 can (8 ounces) DEL MONTE Tomato Sauce
¼ cup red wine (optional)
   Shredded or grated Parmesan cheese

Cook pasta according to package directions; drain. In large saucepan, brown
meat and sausage; drain, reserving 1 tablespoon drippings. Add onion and
garlic to meat, sausage and reserved drippings. Cook over medium-high he:
until tender. Add tomatoes, tomato sauce and wine. Cook, uncovered,
15 minutes, stirring frequently. Serve sauce over hot pasta and top with
Parmesan cheese.   *4 servings (4 cups sau*

Prep & Cook time: 30 minutes

Helpful Hint: *Cook pasta ahead; rinse and drain. Cover and refrigerate. Ju
before serving, heat in microwave or dip in boiling water.*

Chunky Pasta Sauce with Me

CHICKEN PARMESAN

4 half boneless chicken breasts, skinned
2 cans (14½ ounces *each*) DEL MONTE® Italian Recipe
Stewed Tomatoes
2 tablespoons cornstarch
½ teaspoon dried oregano or basil, crushed
¼ teaspoon hot pepper sauce (optional)
¼ cup grated Parmesan cheese

Preheat oven to 425°F. Slightly flatten each chicken breast; place in
11×7-inch baking dish. Cover with foil; bake 20 minutes or until chicken is
no longer pink. Remove foil; drain. Meanwhile, in large saucepan, combine
tomatoes, cornstarch, oregano and pepper sauce. Stir to dissolve cornstarch
Cook, stirring constantly, until thickened. Pour sauce over chicken; top with
cheese. Return to oven; bake, uncovered, 5 minutes or until cheese is melte
Garnish with chopped parsley and serve with rice or pasta, if desired.

4 servir

Prep & Cook time: 30 minutes

Nutrients per serving:			
Calories	228 (14% fat)	Cholesterol	73.0
Fat	3.6 g	Sodium	716.0

SAVORY ZUCCHINI PASTA TOSS

4 ounces bow-tie pasta
1 pound zucchini, sliced (approximately 3 medium)
1 clove garlic, minced
2 tablespoons olive oil
1 can (14½ ounces) DEL MONTE® Pasta Style Chunky
Tomatoes
1½ cups shredded Monterey Jack cheese
1 cup sliced green onions
½ cup grated Parmesan cheese

Cook pasta according to package directions; drain. In large skillet, cook
zucchini and garlic in oil over medium-high heat 3 minutes. Add tomatoes;
cook, uncovered, 5 to 8 minutes, stirring occasionally. Toss with hot pasta,
Jack cheese, green onions and Parmesan cheese. Heat until cheese is melted.
Serve immediately.

6 serving

Prep & Cook time: 25 minutes

Chicken Parmesa

BRUSCHETTA

1 can (14½ ounces) DEL MONTE® Italian Recipe Stewed
   Tomatoes
1 to 2 cloves garlic, crushed
2 tablespoons chopped fresh basil *or* ½ teaspoon dried basil
1 baguette (6 inches) French bread, cut into ½-inch slices
1 tablespoon olive oil

Drain tomatoes reserving liquid. In small saucepan, boil reserved liquid
with garlic, 5 to 6 minutes, stirring occasionally. Remove from heat. Chop
tomatoes; combine with garlic mixture and basil. Brush bread with oil. Broil
until golden. Top with tomato mixture; serve immediately. Garnish with basil
leaves, if desired.   *6 appetizer servings*

Prep time: 5 minutes   **Cook time:** 5 minutes

TOMATO PESTO LASAGNA

8 ounces lasagna noodles (2 inches wide)
1 pound crumbled sausage or ground beef
1 can (14½ ounces) DEL MONTE® Pasta Style Chunky
   Tomatoes
1 can (6 ounces) DEL MONTE Tomato Paste
8 ounces ricotta cheese
1 package (4 ounces) pesto sauce°
2 cups shredded mozzarella cheese

Cook noodles according to package directions; rinse, drain and separate
noodles. In large skillet, brown meat; drain. Stir in tomatoes, tomato paste
and ¾ cup water; mix well. In 2-quart or 9-inch square baking dish, layer
⅓ meat sauce, then ½ each of noodles (cut noodles to fit if necessary), ricotta,
pesto and mozzarella cheese; repeat layers ending with sauce. Top with grated
Parmesan cheese, if desired. Bake at 350°F, 30 minutes or until heated
through.   *6 servings*

Microwave Directions: In 9-inch square microwavable dish, assemble
lasagna as directed above. Cover with plastic wrap; microwave on HIGH 10
minutes, rotating halfway through.

°Available frozen or refrigerated at the supermarket.

Prep time: 20 minutes   **Cook time:** 30 minutes
Microwave cook time: 10 minutes

CHICKEN POMODORO

2 cloves garlic, finely minced
4 half boneless chicken breasts, skinned
⅛ teaspoon crushed red pepper flakes (optional)
1 tablespoon olive oil
1 can (14½ ounces) DEL MONTE® Italian Recipe Stewed
   Tomatoes
2 small zucchini, cut in half lengthwise and sliced crosswise
2 tablespoons thinly sliced fresh basil leaves *or* ½ teaspoon
   dried basil
⅓ cup whipping cream

Rub garlic over chicken. Sprinkle with red pepper. Season with salt and
pepper, if desired. In large skillet, brown chicken in oil over medium-high
heat. Stir in tomatoes, zucchini and basil. Cook, uncovered, over medium-
high heat 15 minutes or until sauce is thickened and chicken is no longer
pink, stirring occasionally. Stir in cream; heat through. *Do not boil.*

4 servi

Prep time: 8 minutes   **Cook time:** 23 minutes

TORTELLINI BAKE PARMESANO

1 package (12 ounces) fresh or frozen cheese tortellini or
   ravioli
½ pound lean ground beef
½ medium onion, finely chopped
2 cloves garlic, minced
½ teaspoon dried oregano, crushed
2 cans (14½ ounces *each*) DEL MONTE® Pasta Style Chunky
   Tomatoes
2 small zucchini, sliced
⅓ cup grated Parmesan cheese

Cook pasta according to package directions; rinse and drain. In large skillet,
brown meat with onion, garlic and oregano; drain. Season with salt and
pepper, if desired. Add tomatoes and zucchini. Cook, uncovered, over
medium-high heat 15 minutes or until thickened, stirring occasionally. In
oiled 2-quart microwavable dish, arrange ½ of pasta; top with ½ of sauce and
½ of cheese. Repeat layers ending with cheese. Cover and microwave on
HIGH 8 to 10 minutes or until heated through, rotating halfway through.

4 servin

Prep & Cook time: 35 minutes

Chicken Pomodor

COUNTRY-STYLE LASAGNA

9 lasagna noodles (2 inches wide)
2 cans (14½ ounces *each*) DEL MONTE® Pasta Style Chunky
   Tomatoes
   Milk
2 tablespoons butter or margarine
3 tablespoons all-purpose flour
1 teaspoon dried basil, crushed
1 cup diced cooked ham
2 cups shredded mozzarella cheese

Cook noodles according to package directions; rinse, drain and separate noodles. Drain tomatoes reserving liquid; pour liquid into measuring cup. Add milk to measure 2 cups. In large saucepan, melt butter; stir in flour and basil. Cook over medium heat 3 minutes, stirring constantly. Stir in reserved liquid; cook until thickened, stirring constantly. Season to taste with salt and pepper, if desired. Stir in tomatoes. Spread thin layer sauce on bottom of 11×2-inch or 2-quart baking dish. Top with 3 noodles and ⅓ each of sauce, ham and cheese; repeat layers twice ending with cheese. Bake, uncovered, at 375°F, 25 minutes. Garnish with Parmesan cheese or green onions, if desired.

6 serving

Prep time: 15 minutes   **Cook time:** 25 minutes

ITALIAN EGGPLANT PARMIGIANA

1 large eggplant, sliced ¼ inch thick
2 eggs, beaten
½ cup dry bread crumbs
1 can (14½ ounces) DEL MONTE® Italian Recipe Stewed
   Tomatoes
1 can (15 ounces) DEL MONTE Tomato Sauce
2 cloves garlic, minced
½ teaspoon dried basil
6 ounces mozzarella cheese, sliced

Dip eggplant slices into eggs, then bread crumbs; arrange in single layer on baking sheet. Broil 4 inches from heat until brown and tender, about 5 minutes per side. *Reduce oven temperature to 350°F.* Place eggplant in 13×9-inch baking dish. Combine tomatoes, tomato sauce, garlic and basil; pour over eggplant and top with cheese. Cover and bake at 350°F, 30 minutes or until heated through. Sprinkle with grated Parmesan cheese, if desired.

4 main dish servings (6 side dish servings

Prep time: 15 minutes   **Cook time:** 30 minutes

Country-Style Lasagna

SKILLET SPAGHETTI AND SAUSAGE

¼ pound mild or hot Italian sausage links, sliced
½ pound ground beef
¼ teaspoon dried oregano, crushed
4 ounces spaghetti, broken in half
1 can (14½ ounces) DEL MONTE® Pasta Style Chunky
    Tomatoes
1 can (8 ounces) DEL MONTE Tomato Sauce
1½ cups sliced fresh mushrooms
2 stalks celery, sliced

In large skillet, brown sausage over medium-high heat. Add beef and oregan
season to taste with salt and pepper, if desired. Cook, stirring occasionally,
until beef is browned; drain. Add pasta, 1 cup water, tomatoes, tomato sauce
mushrooms and celery. Bring to boil, stirring occasionally. Reduce heat; cove
and simmer 12 to 14 minutes or until spaghetti is tender. Garnish with grated
Parmesan cheese and chopped parsley, if desired. Serve immediately.

4 to 6 serving

Prep time: 5 minutes   **Cook time:** 30 minutes

KIDS   Easy recipe for kids and parents to make together.

EGGPLANT PASTA BAKE

4 ounces bow-tie pasta
1 pound eggplant, diced
1 clove garlic, minced
¼ cup olive oil
1½ cups shredded Monterey Jack cheese
1 cup sliced green onions
½ cup grated Parmesan cheese
1 can (14½ ounces) DEL MONTE® Pasta Style Chunky
    Tomatoes

Preheat oven to 350°F. Cook pasta according to package directions; drain.
In large skillet, cook eggplant and garlic in oil over medium-high heat until
tender. Toss eggplant with cooked pasta, 1 cup Jack cheese, green onions
and Parmesan cheese. Place in greased 9-inch square baking dish. Top with
tomatoes and remaining ½ cup Jack cheese. Bake 15 minutes or until heated
through.   *6 serving*

Prep & Cook time: 30 minutes

MELET ITALIANO

medium mushrooms, sliced
teaspoon dried oregano
teaspoons butter
can (14½ ounces) DEL MONTE® Italian Recipe Stewed
　Tomatoes
eggs, beaten
cup shredded mozzarella cheese
cup diced pepperoni or ham
green onions, sliced

large saucepan, cook mushrooms and oregano in 1 teaspoon butter. Add
matoes. Cook, uncovered, over medium-high heat 10 minutes or until
ckened; set aside. In large skillet, heat remaining 3 teaspoons butter over
edium-high heat. Beat together eggs and ¼ cup water; season with salt and
pper, if desired. Pour into skillet. Once eggs begin to set, run spatula
ound edge of pan, lifting to allow uncooked eggs to flow underneath. When
gs are set, sprinkle left side with cheese, pepperoni and green onions. Fold
ht half over filling. When cheese melts, remove to serving platter. Pour
ushroom-tomato sauce over omelet. *2 servings*

rep & Cook time: 15 minutes

elpful Hint: *A nonstick skillet makes this especially easy.*

PICY PEPPERONI PIZZA

4 (6-inch) prepared, pre-baked pizza crusts
1 can (14½ ounces) DEL MONTE® Pizza Style Chunky
　Tomatoes
2 cups shredded mozzarella cheese
2 ounces sliced pepperoni
8 pitted ripe olives, sliced
2 tablespoons sliced green onions

reheat oven to 450°F. Place crusts on baking sheet. Spread tomatoes evenly
ver crusts. Layer ½ of cheese, then the pepperoni, olives and green onions.
op with remaining cheese. Bake 6 to 8 minutes or until hot and bubbly.
4 servings

rep time: 7 minutes　　　　　　**Cook time:** 8 minutes

KIDS　　Easy recipe for kids and parents to make together.

GARDEN PRIMAVERA PASTA

6 ounces bow-tie pasta
1 jar (6 ounces) marinated artichoke hearts
2 cloves garlic, minced
½ teaspoon dried rosemary, crushed
1 green pepper, cut into thin strips
1 large carrot, cut into 3-inch julienne strips
1 medium zucchini, cut into 3-inch julienne strips
1 can (14½ ounces) DEL MONTE® Pasta Style Chunky
    Tomatoes
12 small pitted ripe olives (optional)

Cook pasta according to package directions; drain. Drain artichokes reservin
marinade. Toss pasta in 3 tablespoons artichoke marinade; set aside. Cut
artichoke hearts into halves. In large skillet, cook garlic and rosemary in
1 tablespoon artichoke marinade. Add remaining ingredients, except pasta
and artichokes. Cook, uncovered, over medium-high heat 4 to 5 minutes or
until vegetables are tender-crisp and sauce is thickened. Add artichoke hear
Spoon over pasta. Serve with grated Parmesan cheese, if desired.

4 servin

Prep time: 15 minutes   **Cook time:** 10 minutes

TOMATO RISOTTO PRONTO

1 can (14½ ounces) DEL MONTE® Italian Recipe Stewed
    Tomatoes
2 large mushrooms, sliced
1 tablespoon olive oil
1 cup uncooked long grain white rice
1 clove garlic, minced
⅛ to ¼ teaspoon pepper
1¼ cups chicken broth
¼ cup grated Parmesan cheese

Drain tomatoes reserving liquid; pour liquid into measuring cup. Add water t
measure 1⅔ cups. In large saucepan, brown mushrooms in oil. Add rice, garli
and pepper; cook 2 minutes. Add reserved liquid and tomatoes; bring to boil.
Cover and cook over low heat 18 minutes. Remove cover; increase heat to
medium. Gradually stir in ½ cup broth. When liquid is gone, gradually add
another ½ cup broth, adding remaining ¼ cup broth when liquid is gone. Add
cheese. Rice should be tender-firm but creamy. Serve immediately.

4 to 6 serving

Prep time: 8 minutes   **Cook time:** 32 minutes

Garden Primavera Past

SICILIAN SKILLET CHICKEN

4 half boneless chicken breasts, skinned
6 tablespoons grated Parmesan cheese
3 tablespoons all-purpose flour
2 tablespoons olive oil
1 cup sliced mushrooms
½ medium onion, finely chopped
½ teaspoon dried rosemary, crushed
1 can (14½ ounces) DEL MONTE® Italian Recipe Stewed
   Tomatoes

Slightly flatten each chicken breast. Coat breasts with 4 tablespoons cheese
and then flour. Season with salt and pepper, if desired. Heat oil in large skill'
over medium-high heat. Cook chicken until no longer pink, turning once.
Remove to serving dish; keep warm. In same skillet, cook mushrooms, onion
and rosemary until tender. Add tomatoes; cook, uncovered, over medium-
high heat until thickened. Spoon over chicken; top with remaining
2 tablespoons cheese. Serve with pasta and garnish with chopped parsley,
if desired.   *4 servin*

Prep time: 5 minutes   **Cook time:** 25 minutes

CALZONE ITALIANO

1 loaf frozen bread dough, thawed°
1 can (15 ounces) DEL MONTE® Chopped Spinach
8 ounces ricotta cheese
1 can (14½ ounces) DEL MONTE Pizza Style Chunky
   Tomatoes
1½ cups shredded mozzarella cheese

Preheat oven to 400°F. Divide dough into four portions. On floured board,
roll dough into 7-inch rounds. Drain spinach, squeezing out excess liquid.
Spread half of each round with ricotta cheese, tomatoes, spinach and
mozzarella cheese. Fold each round in half, folding dough over filling;
pinch edges to seal. Place on baking sheet. Brush with olive oil, if desired.
Bake 15 to 20 minutes or until golden.   *4 serving*

*°Refrigerated pizza dough may be used; prepare according to package
directions.*

Prep time: 15 minutes   **Cook time:** 20 minutes

Sicilian Skillet Chicke

PESTO CHICKEN PIZZA

1 (12-inch) prepared, pre-baked pizza crust°
¼ cup pesto sauce°°
1 can (14½ ounces) DEL MONTE® Pizza Style Chunky
    Tomatoes
2 cups shredded mozzarella cheese
1½ cups diced cooked chicken
1 small red or green pepper, thinly sliced
1 small zucchini, thinly sliced
5 medium mushrooms, thinly sliced

Preheat oven to 450°F. Place crust on baking sheet. Spread pesto evenly ove
crust. Top with tomatoes, cheese and remaining ingredients. Bake 10 minut
or until hot and bubbly. Garnish with grated Parmesan cheese and chopped
fresh basil, if desired.   *4 to 6 servin*

°*Substitute 4 (6-inch) prepared, pre-baked pizza crusts. Refrigerated or froz
pizza dough may also be used; prepare and bake according to package
directions.*

°°*Available frozen or refrigerated at the supermarket.*

Prep time: 10 minutes   **Cook time:** 10 minutes

Helpful Hint: *Toss vegetables in 1 tablespoon olive oil, if desired.*

ITALIAN-STYLE MEAT LOAF

1 pound lean ground beef
6 ounces Italian sausage, casings removed, or spicy bulk
    sausage
1 can (14½ ounces) DEL MONTE® Italian Recipe Stewed
    Tomatoes
1 cup dry bread crumbs
½ cup chopped onion
½ cup chopped green pepper
1 egg, beaten

In large bowl, combine all ingredients; mix well. Place in 8×4½-inch glass loa
pan. Bake at 350°F, 65 to 75 minutes or until no longer pink in center.

                                                     6 serving

Prep time: 10 minutes   **Cook time:** 75 minutes

Helpful Hint: *For metal loaf pan, increase oven temperature to 375°F.*

Pesto Chicken Pizz

MILANO SHRIMP FETTUCINE

4 ounces egg or spinach fettucine
½ pound medium shrimp, peeled and deveined
1 clove garlic, minced
1 tablespoon olive oil
1 can (14½ ounces) DEL MONTE® Pasta Style Chunky
    Tomatoes
½ cup whipping cream
¼ cup sliced green onions

Cook pasta according to package directions; drain. In large skillet, cook shrimp and garlic in oil over medium-high heat until shrimp are pink and opaque. Stir in tomatoes; simmer 5 minutes. Blend in cream and green onions; heat through. *Do not boil.* Serve over hot pasta.   *3 to 4 servin*

Prep & Cook time: 20 minutes

CALICO MINESTRONE
SOUP   LOW FAT

2 cans (14 ounces *each*) chicken broth
¼ cup uncooked small shell pasta
1 can (14½ ounces) DEL MONTE® Italian Recipe Stewed
    Tomatoes
1 can (8¾ ounces) or 1 cup kidney beans, drained
½ cup chopped cooked chicken or beef
1 carrot, cubed
1 stalk celery, sliced
½ teaspoon dried basil, crushed

In large saucepan, bring broth to boil; stir in pasta and boil 5 minutes. Add remaining ingredients. Reduce heat; cover and simmer 20 minutes. Garnish with grated Parmesan cheese, if desired.

Approximately 6 servings (1 cup each

Prep time: 5 minutes   **Cook time:** 25 minutes

Nutrients per serving:			
Calories	103 (16% fat)	Cholesterol	12.0 m
Fat	1.9 g	Sodium	754.6 m

KIDS   Easy recipe for kids and parents to make together.

Milano Shrimp Fettucin

CHICKEN PESTO MOZZARELLA

6 to 8 ounces linguine or corkscrew pasta
4 half boneless chicken breasts, skinned
1 tablespoon olive oil
1 can (14½ ounces) DEL MONTE® Pasta Style Chunky
   Tomatoes
½ medium onion, chopped
⅓ cup sliced ripe olives
4 teaspoons pesto sauce°
¼ cup shredded skim-milk mozzarella cheese

Cook pasta according to package directions; drain. Meanwhile, season chick
with salt and pepper, if desired. In large skillet, brown chicken in oil over
medium-high heat. Add tomatoes, onion and olives; bring to boil. Cover and
cook 8 minutes over medium heat. Remove cover; cook over medium-high
heat about 8 minutes or until chicken is no longer pink. Spread 1 teaspoon
pesto over each breast; top with cheese. Cook, covered, until cheese melts.
Serve over pasta.   *4 servir*

°*Available frozen or refrigerated at the supermarket.*

Prep time: 10 minutes   **Cook time:** 25 minutes

Nutrients per serving:			
Calories	402 (25% fat)	Cholesterol	112.3
Fat	10.9 g	Sodium	436.0

THREE CHEESE PIZZA

4 (6-inch) prepared, pre-baked pizza crusts *or* 4 (6-inch) pita
   pocket breads
1 can (14½ ounces) DEL MONTE® Pizza Style Chunky
   Tomatoes
¾ cup shredded mozzarella cheese
½ cup shredded Swiss cheese
3 tablespoons grated Parmesan cheese

Preheat oven to 450°F. Place crusts on baking sheet. Spread tomatoes evenly
over crusts. Top with cheeses. Bake 6 to 8 minutes or until hot and bubbly.
                                                         4 serving

Prep time: 12 minutes   **Cook time:** 8 minutes

Variation: *Substitute 8 toasted English muffin halves for pizza crusts.*

Chicken Pesto Mozzarell

Mediterranean Fare

Experience the exciting flavors of Greece, Morocco and other Mediterranean countries in these delicious recipes.

CHICKEN MOROCCO

LOW FAT/LOW SALT

1 cup uncooked bulgur wheat
4 chicken thighs, skinned
½ medium onion, chopped
1 tablespoon olive oil
1 can (14½ ounces) DEL MONTE® Original Recipe Stewed
    Tomatoes (No Salt Added)
½ cup DEL MONTE Prune Juice
6 DEL MONTE Pitted Prunes, diced
¼ teaspoon ground allspice

In large saucepan, bring 1½ cups water to boil; add bulgur. Cover and cook over low heat 20 minutes or until tender. Meanwhile, season chicken with salt-free herb seasoning, if desired. In large skillet, brown chicken with onion in oil over medium-high heat; drain. Stir in tomatoes, prune juice, prunes and allspice. Cover and cook 10 minutes over medium heat. Remove cover; cook over medium-high heat 10 to 12 minutes or until sauce thickens and chicken is no longer pink, turning chicken and stirring sauce occasionally. Serve chicken and sauce over bulgur. Garnish with chopped parsley, if desired.

4 serving

Prep time: 5 minutes   **Cook time:** 30 minutes

Nutrients per serving:			
Calories	334 (25% fat)	Cholesterol	49.0 m
Fat	9.7 g	Sodium	95.0 m

Chicken Morocc

LAMB SALAD WITH TOMATOES AND FETA

¾ pound boneless lamb chops (1 inch thick)
3 tablespoons olive oil
1 can (14½ ounces) DEL MONTE® Original Recipe Stewed
   Tomatoes
3 tablespoons red wine vinegar
2 to 3 tablespoons minced fresh mint *or* ½ teaspoon dried
   mint
½ medium red onion, thinly sliced
   Shredded lettuce
½ cup crumbled feta cheese

Season meat with salt and pepper, if desired. In large skillet, heat
1 tablespoon oil over medium-high heat. Cook meat in oil about 4 minutes o
each side or until cooked as desired; cut crosswise into thin slices. Drain
tomatoes reserving ⅓ cup liquid. Combine reserved liquid with vinegar, mint
and remaining 2 tablespoons oil. Toss meat slices, tomatoes and onion with
dressing; arrange over lettuce. Top with cheese and garnish with chopped
parsley, if desired. *4 servin*

Prep time: 12 minutes   **Cook time:** 8 minutes

Variation: *Grill lamb over hot coals instead of pan-frying.*

COUNTRY MEDITERRANEAN PILAF

1 medium onion, chopped
1 clove garlic, crushed
2 tablespoons butter or margarine
¾ cup uncooked long grain white rice
¼ cup crushed vermicelli or spaghetti
1 can (14½ ounces) DEL MONTE® Original Recipe Stewed
   Tomatoes
   Chicken broth

In large skillet, cook onion and garlic in butter until tender. Stir in rice and
pasta; cook until browned. Drain tomatoes reserving liquid; pour liquid into
measuring cup. Add broth to measure 2 cups. Stir tomatoes and liquid into
onion mixture. Bring to boil; cover and simmer over medium heat 15 minutes
or until rice is tender. Garnish with toasted sliced almonds and chopped
parsley, if desired. *4 to 6 servings*

Prep time: 7 minutes   **Cook time:** 23 minutes

Lamb Salad with Tomatoes and Feta

MOROCCAN LAMB OR BEEF

LOW FAT

¾ pound ground lamb or beef
1 cup chopped onion
1 can (14½ ounces) DEL MONTE® Original Recipe Stewed
    Tomatoes
⅓ cup chopped DEL MONTE Dried Apricots
¼ cup DEL MONTE Seedless Raisins
1 teaspoon ground cinnamon
¼ teaspoon ground cloves
1 banana, sliced
2 cups hot cooked rice, brown rice or bulgur

In large skillet, brown meat over medium-high heat. Add onion and cook unt
tender; drain. Add tomatoes, apricots, raisins, cinnamon and cloves. Cover
and simmer 10 minutes. Season with salt and pepper, if desired. Add banana
Heat through. Serve over rice. Top with plain yogurt and chopped peanuts, i
desired.

4 to 5 servin

Nutrients per serving:			
Calories	383 (18% fat)	Cholesterol	69.3 m
Fat	7.9 g	Sodium	294.0 m

Variations: *Substitute DEL MONTE Mixed Dried Fruit for apricots. Lamb
may be served in pita bread.*

BARCELONA GAZPACHO

LOW FAT

1 can (14½ ounces) DEL MONTE® Mexican Recipe Stewed
    Tomatoes
1 can (8 ounces) DEL MONTE Tomato Sauce
½ cup mild green chile salsa
2 tablespoons lime juice
2 teaspoons olive oil
1 teaspoon sugar
⅛ cup chopped cucumber
⅛ cup chopped green pepper
⅛ cup sliced green onions

continued

rain tomatoes reserving liquid; chop tomatoes. Combine reserved liquid,
of chopped tomatoes, tomato sauce, salsa, lime juice, oil and sugar.
ombine remaining chopped tomatoes with cucumber, green pepper and
een onions. Chill until ready to serve. To serve, ladle liquid into 4 soup
wls. Top with chopped vegetables. Garnish with low fat sour cream and
antro, if desired.

4 servings

ep time: 15 minutes   **Chill time:** 30 minutes

utrients per serving:

lories	84 (29% fat)	Cholesterol	0.0 mg
t	3.2 g	Sodium	715.0 mg

ABBOULI LAMB SANDWICH

LOW FAT

1 can (14½ ounces) DEL MONTE® Original Recipe Stewed
    Tomatoes
½ cup bulgur wheat, uncooked
½ cups cooked diced lamb or beef
¾ cup diced cucumber
3 tablespoons minced fresh mint or parsley
1 tablespoon lemon juice
1 tablespoon olive oil
3 pita breads, cut into halves

)rain tomatoes reserving liquid; pour liquid into measuring cup. Add water, if
eeded, to measure ¾ cup. In small saucepan, bring liquid to boil; add bulgur.
Cover and simmer over low heat 20 minutes or until tender. Cool. Chop
omatoes. In medium bowl, combine tomatoes, meat, cucumber, mint, lemon
iice and oil. Stir in cooled bulgur. Season with salt and pepper, if desired.
poon about ½ cup tabbouli into each half pita bread.

6 sandwiches (½ pita each)

Prep & Cook time: 25 minutes   **Chill time:** 30 minutes

Nutrients per serving:

Calories	239 (25% fat)	Cholesterol	34.8 mg
Fat	6.7 g	Sodium	342.5 mg

MEDITERRANEAN PASTA

6 to 8 ounces vermicelli
2 half boneless chicken breasts, skinned and cut into
    1½ × ½-inch strips
4 slices bacon, diced
1 can (14½ ounces) DEL MONTE® Pasta Style Chunky
    Tomatoes
1 can (15 ounces) DEL MONTE Tomato Sauce
½ teaspoon dried rosemary, crushed
1 package (9 ounces) frozen artichoke hearts, thawed
½ cup pitted ripe olives, sliced lengthwise

Cook pasta according to package directions; drain. Season chicken with salt
and pepper, if desired. In large skillet, cook bacon until almost crisp; add
chicken. Brown chicken on both sides over medium-high heat; drain. Stir in
tomatoes, tomato sauce and rosemary. Cook, uncovered, 15 minutes, stirring
occasionally. Add artichokes and olives; heat through. Just before serving,
spoon sauce over hot pasta. Garnish with crumbled feta cheese and chopped
parsley, if desired.   *4 to 6 serving*

Prep time: 5 minutes   **Cook time:** 30 minutes

Helpful Hint: *Cook pasta ahead; rinse and drain. Cover and refrigerate. Just
before serving, heat in microwave or dip in boiling water.*

CAPONATA

1 pound eggplant, cut into ½-inch cubes
3 large cloves garlic, minced
¼ cup olive oil
1 can (14½ ounces) DEL MONTE® Italian Recipe Stewed
    Tomatoes
1 medium green pepper, finely chopped
1 can (2¼ ounces) chopped ripe olives, drained
2 tablespoons lemon juice
1 teaspoon dried basil, crushed
1 baguette French bread, cut into ¼-inch slices

In large skillet, cook eggplant and garlic in oil over medium heat 5 minutes.
Season with salt and pepper, if desired. Stir in remaining ingredients except
bread. Cook, uncovered, 10 minutes or until thickened. Cover and chill. Serve
with bread.   *Approximately 4½ cups*

Prep time: 10 minutes   **Cook time:** 15 minutes
Chill time: 2 hours

Mediterranean Pasta

GREEK-STYLE PIZZA

1 (12-inch) prepared, pre-baked pizza crust°
1 can (14½ ounces) DEL MONTE® Pizza Style Chunky
    Tomatoes
1 cup shredded mozzarella cheese
1 cup crumbled feta cheese
1 small red onion, thinly sliced
¼ cup chopped fresh basil leaves or fresh spinach
¼ cup sliced ripe olives
¼ teaspoon dried oregano, crushed

Preheat oven to 450°F. Place crust on baking sheet. Spread tomatoes evenly
over crust. Top with cheeses, onion, basil, olives and oregano. Bake
10 minutes or until hot and bubbly. Garnish with additional basil, if desired.

4 to 6 servings

°*Substitute 4 (6-inch) prepared, pre-baked pizza crusts. Refrigerated or frozen
pizza dough may also be used; prepare and bake according to package
directions.*

Prep time: 10 minutes   **Cook time:** 10 minutes

CHICKEN ATHENA

1 pound boneless chicken,° skinned and cut into cubes
1 tablespoon olive oil
1 medium onion, cut into chunks
1 can (14½ ounces) DEL MONTE® Original Recipe Stewed
    Tomatoes
1 jar (6 ounces) marinated artichoke hearts
¼ teaspoon dried rosemary, crushed
⅓ cup crumbled feta cheese (optional)

In large skillet, brown chicken in oil over medium-high heat; add onion and
cook 2 minutes. Stir in tomatoes, marinade from artichokes and rosemary;
cook over medium heat 10 to 15 minutes or until thickened, stirring
frequently. Stir in artichoke hearts; heat through. Top with feta cheese.
Garnish with chopped parsley, if desired.

4 to 6 servings

°*Substitute fresh turkey for chicken.*

Prep time: 5 minutes   **Cook time:** 22 minutes

QUICK MEDITERRANEAN FISH

1 medium onion, sliced
2 tablespoons olive oil
1 clove garlic, crushed
1 can (14½ ounces) DEL MONTE® Italian Recipe Stewed
    Tomatoes
3 to 4 tablespoons medium green chile salsa
¼ teaspoon ground cinnamon
1½ pounds firm fish (such as halibut, red snapper or sea bass)
12 stuffed green olives, halved crosswise

Microwave Directions: In 1½-quart microwavable dish, combine onion, oil
and garlic. Cover and microwave on HIGH 3 minutes; drain. Stir in tomatoes
salsa and cinnamon. Top with fish and olives. Cover and microwave on HIGH
3 to 4 minutes or until fish flakes easily with fork. Garnish with chopped
parsley, if desired. *4 to 6 servings*

Prep time: 7 minutes   **Microwave cook time:** 7 minutes

LAMB WITH YOGURT MINT SAUCE

LOW FAT

¾ pound boneless lamb or beef, cut into ¼-inch cubes
1 tablespoon olive oil
1 medium onion, cut into wedges
1 can (14½ ounces) DEL MONTE® Pasta Style Chunky
    Tomatoes
1 to 2 tablespoons chutney
1 teaspoon ground cumin
⅓ cup nonfat plain yogurt
1 tablespoon chopped fresh mint *or* 1 teaspoon dried mint
4 cups hot cooked pasta

In large skillet, brown meat in oil over medium-high heat. Stir in onion and
cook 3 to 4 minutes. Add tomatoes, chutney and cumin; cook until thickened.
Combine yogurt with mint. Spoon meat mixture over hot pasta and top with
yogurt mixture. *4 servings*

Prep time: 5 minutes   **Cook time:** 12 minutes

Nutrients per Serving:			
Calories	483 (27% fat)	Cholesterol	131.0 mg
Fat	14.2 g	Sodium	353.0 mg

Quick Mediterranean Fish

36   **MEDITERRANEAN FARE**

Asian Dishes

Discover the ancient secrets of the Far East with these quick and easy dishes from Asia.

CHICKEN SALAD CANTON

1 cup fresh Chinese snow peas *or* 1 package (6 ounces) frozen snow peas, thawed
1 can (14½ ounces) **DEL MONTE®** Original Recipe Stewed Tomatoes
3 tablespoons vegetable oil
3 tablespoons cider vinegar
1 tablespoon low-salt soy sauce
4 cups shredded cabbage or iceberg lettuce
1 cup cubed cooked chicken
⅓ cup packed cilantro, chopped *or* ⅓ cup sliced green onions

Dip fresh snow peas in boiling water 30 seconds (do not dip frozen snow peas); cool. Drain tomatoes reserving ¼ cup liquid. Combine reserved liquid with oil, vinegar and soy sauce. Toss soy dressing and tomatoes with remaining ingredients. Season to taste with pepper, if desired. Garnish with sliced green onions and toasted sesame seeds, if desired.

2 main dish servings (4 side dish servings

Prep time: 15 minutes

Chicken Salad Canton

TOMATO GINGER BEEF

2 tablespoons dry sherry
1 tablespoon soy sauce
2 cloves garlic, crushed
1 teaspoon minced gingerroot *or* ¼ teaspoon ground ginger
1 pound flank steak, thinly sliced
1 tablespoon cornstarch
1 tablespoon vegetable oil
1 can (14¼ ounces) DEL MONTE® Original Recipe Stewed
   Tomatoes
   Hot cooked rice

Combine sherry, soy sauce, garlic and ginger; toss with meat. Stir in cornstarch; mix well. In large skillet, cook meat mixture in oil over high heat until browned, stirring constantly. Add tomatoes; cook over high heat until thickened, stirring frequently, about 5 minutes. Serve over hot cooked rice. Garnish with sliced green onions, if desired.   *4 to 6 servin*

Prep time: 10 minutes   **Cook time:** 12 minutes

Helpful Hint: *Partially freeze meat for easier slicing.*

COUNTRY JAPANESE
NOODLE SOUP   LOW FAT

1 can (14½ ounces) DEL MONTE® Original Recipe Stewed
   Tomatoes
1 can (14 ounces) low-salt chicken broth
3 ounces linguine
1 to 1½ teaspoons minced gingerroot *or* ¼ teaspoon ground
   ginger
2 teaspoons low-salt soy sauce
¼ pound sirloin steak, cut crosswise into thin strips
5 green onions, cut into thin 1-inch slivers
4 ounces firm tofu, cut into small cubes

large saucepan, combine tomatoes, broth, pasta, ginger and soy sauce
with 1¾ cups water; bring to boil. Cook, uncovered, over medium-high heat
minutes. Add meat, green onions and tofu; cook 4 minutes or until pasta
tender. Season to taste with pepper and additional soy sauce, if desired.

4 servings (1¼ cups each)

Prep time: 10 minutes   **Cook time:** 15 minutes

Nutrients per serving:

Calories	220 (26% fat)	Cholesterol	39.5 mg
Fat	6.6 g	Sodium	535.0 mg

THAI CHICKEN CURRY

**1 can (14½ ounces) DEL MONTE® Original Recipe Stewed
    Tomatoes
2 teaspoons curry powder
1 teaspoon sugar
½ teaspoon grated lemon peel
¼ to ½ teaspoon minced jalapeño chile
1 pound boneless, skinless chicken, cut into ¾-inch cubes
¾ cup coconut milk°
3 tablespoons thinly sliced fresh basil leaves *or* 1 teaspoon
    dried basil
    Hot cooked rice**

In large skillet, combine tomatoes, curry, sugar, lemon peel and jalapeño.
Cook, uncovered, over medium-high heat 7 minutes or until thickened,
stirring occasionally. Season chicken with salt and pepper, if desired. Add
chicken, coconut milk and basil to skillet. Cover and cook over medium heat
8 minutes or until chicken is no longer pink. Serve over hot cooked rice.

3 to 4 servings

°*If coconut milk is not available, omit sugar. Add 3 tablespoons shredded
coconut to tomatoes. Substitute ½ cup whipping cream for coconut milk; add
after chicken is done. Cook, uncovered, over low heat until heated through.*

Prep & Cook time: 25 minutes

CHICKEN CURRY BOMBAY

1 medium onion, cut into wedges
2 cloves garlic, minced
2 teaspoons curry powder
1 tablespoon olive oil
2 half boneless chicken breasts, skinned and sliced ¼ inch
    thick
1 can (14½ ounces) DEL MONTE® Original Recipe Stewed
    Tomatoes
⅓ cup DEL MONTE Seedless Raisins
1 can (16 ounces) DEL MONTE Whole New Potatoes,
    drained and cut into chunks
1 can (16 ounces) DEL MONTE Blue Lake Cut Green
    Beans, drained

In large skillet, cook onion, garlic and curry in oil until tender, stirring occasionally. Stir in chicken, tomatoes and raisins; bring to boil. Cover and simmer over medium heat 8 minutes. Add potatoes and green beans. Cook, uncovered, 5 minutes, stirring occasionally. Season with salt and pepper, if desired.   *4 serving*

Prep time: 10 minutes   **Cook time:** 18 minutes

Nutrients per serving:

Calories	233 (17% fat)	Cholesterol	34.0 m
Fat	4.7 g	Sodium	643.0 m

PEANUT CHICKEN

1 (3-pound) broiler-fryer chicken, cut up
2 teaspoons vegetable oil
1 can (14½ ounces) DEL MONTE® Original Recipe Stewed
    Tomatoes, coarsely chopped
3 tablespoons chunky peanut butter
2 cloves garlic, crushed
1 teaspoon grated gingerroot
1 teaspoon soy sauce
⅛ to ¼ teaspoon red pepper flakes

In large skillet, cook chicken in oil about 25 minutes or until no longer pink; drain. Set chicken aside and keep warm. In same skillet, add undrained tomatoes and remaining ingredients. Simmer 3 minutes. Add chicken; cook 2 minutes or until heated through, turning once. Garnish with chopped peanuts and cilantro, if desired.   *4 to 6 servings*

Prep time: 3 minutes   **Cook time:** 30 minutes

Chicken Curry Bombay

FISH CAKES WITH THAI SALSA

**2 cans (14½ ounces *each*) DEL MONTE® Original Recipe
   Stewed Tomatoes**
¾ cup sliced green onions
1 tablespoon minced gingerroot
¼ teaspoon red pepper flakes
⅓ cup chopped cilantro
**3½ cups cooked, flaked fish (about 1¾ to 2 pounds uncooked
   halibut, salmon or snapper)**
2 eggs, beaten
½ cup Italian seasoned dry bread crumbs
¼ cup mayonnaise
1 to 2 tablespoons butter

Drain tomatoes reserving liquid; chop tomatoes. In medium saucepan,
combine tomatoes with ½ cup green onions, ginger, red pepper and reserved
liquid. Cook, uncovered, over high heat until thickened, stirring occasionally.
Add cilantro. Cool. In medium bowl, combine fish, eggs, crumbs, mayonnaise
remaining ¼ cup green onions and ⅓ cup tomato salsa mixture. Season with
pepper, if desired. Form into 16 patties. Melt butter in large skillet over high
heat. Reduce heat to medium-low; cook patties about 3 minutes per side or
until golden brown. Serve over salad greens, if desired. Top with salsa. Drizzle
with Oriental sesame oil, if desired.   *16 (2½-inch) cake*

Prep & Cook time: 35 minutes

Helpful Hint: *To cook fish, place in microwavable dish; cover and microwave
on HIGH 7 to 9 minutes or until fish flakes with fork, rotating twice; drain.*

Fish Cakes with Thai Salsa

SWEET AND SOUR CHICKEN

6 chicken thighs
2 teaspoons vegetable oil
1 can (8¼ ounces) DEL MONTE® Pineapple Chunks
1 can (14½ ounces) DEL MONTE Original Recipe Stewed
    Tomatoes
3 tablespoons sugar
1 tablespoon cider vinegar
1 teaspoon soy sauce
1 teaspoon grated gingerroot *or* ½ teaspoon ground ginger
2 teaspoons cornstarch
½ green pepper, cubed
    Hot cooked rice

In large skillet, cook chicken in oil over medium-high heat about 15 minutes
or until no longer pink, turning once; drain. Drain pineapple reserving syrup.
In medium saucepan, combine reserved syrup, tomatoes, sugar, vinegar, soy
sauce and ginger; simmer 10 minutes. Combine cornstarch with 2 tablespoon
water. Add cornstarch mixture, pineapple and green pepper to tomato
mixture; cook until thickened. Pour over chicken; cook 5 minutes, turning
chicken. Serve over hot cooked rice. Garnish with green onions, if desired.

4 serving.

Prep time: 3 minutes   **Cook time:** 35 minutes

TOMATO GINGER CHUTNEY

1 tablespoon minced gingerroot *or* ½ teaspoon ground
    ginger
2 cloves garlic, minced
½ teaspoon ground cinnamon
    Dash cayenne pepper
1 teaspoon vegetable oil
1 can (14½ ounces) DEL MONTE® Cajun Recipe Stewed
    Tomatoes
¼ cup firmly packed brown sugar
¼ cup cider vinegar

In small saucepan, cook ginger, garlic, cinnamon and cayenne in oil. Add
tomatoes, sugar and vinegar. Cook, uncovered, over medium-high heat
15 minutes, stirring occasionally. Reduce heat; cook 5 minutes or until
thickened. Serve with poultry, beef or lamb.   *Approximately ¾ cup*

Prep time: 5 minutes   **Cook time:** 20 minutes

Sweet and Sour Chicken

French Cuisine

From country bistro cooking to classic French cuisine—preparing an outstanding meal has never been easier!

TOMATO FRENCH ONION SOUP

    4 medium onions, chopped
    2 tablespoons butter or margarine
    1 can (14½ ounces) DEL MONTE® Italian Recipe Stewed
        Tomatoes
    1 can (10½ ounces) condensed beef consommé
    ¼ cup dry sherry
    4 slices toasted French bread
 1½ cups shredded Swiss cheese
    ¼ cup grated Parmesan cheese

In large saucepan, cook onions in butter about 10 minutes. Drain tomatoes reserving liquid. Chop tomatoes. Add tomatoes, reserved liquid, 2 cups water, consommé and sherry. Bring to boil, skimming off foam. Reduce heat and simmer 10 minutes. Place soup in four broilerproof bowls; top with bread and cheeses. Broil until cheese is melted and golden.

4 servings (1¼ cups each)

Prep time: 5 minutes   **Cook time:** 30 minutes

Helpful Hint: *If broilerproof bowls are not available, place soup in ovenproof bowls and bake at 350°F, 10 minutes.*

Tomato French Onion Soup

COQ AU VIN

4 thin slices bacon, cut into ½-inch pieces
6 chicken thighs, skinned
¾ teaspoon dried thyme, crushed
1 large onion, coarsely chopped
4 cloves garlic, minced
½ pound small red potatoes, quartered
10 mushrooms, quartered
1 can (14½ ounces) DEL MONTE® Italian Recipe Stewed
    Tomatoes
1½ cups dry red wine

In 4-quart heavy saucepan, cook bacon until just starting to brown. Sprinkle chicken with thyme; season with salt and pepper, if desired. Add chicken to pan; brown over medium-high heat. Add onion and garlic. Cook 2 minutes; drain. Add potatoes, mushrooms, tomatoes and wine. Cook, uncovered, over medium-high heat about 25 minutes or until potatoes are tender and sauce thickens, stirring occasionally. Garnish with chopped parsley, if desired.

4 to 6 serving

Prep & Cook time: 45 minutes

PIZZA AUBERGINE

1 small eggplant (about ¾ pound), halved and thinly sliced
1 medium onion, halved and sliced
2 tablespoons vegetable oil
2 cups sliced mushrooms
2 cloves garlic, minced
1 (12-inch) prepared, pre-baked pizza crust°
1 can (14½ ounces) DEL MONTE® Pizza Style Chunky
    Tomatoes
2 cups shredded mozzarella cheese

Preheat oven to 450°F. In large skillet, cook eggplant and onion in oil over medium-high heat until tender. Add mushrooms and garlic and cook 5 minutes; drain. Place crust on baking sheet. Spread tomatoes evenly over crust. Top with cheese and eggplant mixture. Bake 10 minutes or until hot and bubbly.

4 to 6 serving

°*Substitute 4 (6-inch) prepared, pre-baked pizza crusts. Refrigerated or frozen pizza dough may also be used; prepare and bake according to package directions.*

Prep time: 20 minutes   **Cook time:** 10 minutes

Coq au Vin

DIJON LAMB STEW

LOW FAT

½ pound boneless lamb, cut into small pieces°
½ medium onion, chopped
½ teaspoon dried rosemary
1 tablespoon olive oil
1 can (14½ ounces) DEL MONTE® Italian Recipe Stewed
   Tomatoes
1 carrot, julienne cut
1 tablespoon Dijon mustard
1 can (15 ounces) white beans or pinto beans, drained

In large skillet, brown meat with onion and rosemary in oil over medium-high heat, stirring occasionally. Season with salt and pepper, if desired. Add tomatoes, carrot and mustard. Cover and cook over medium heat, 10 minutes; add beans. Cook, uncovered, over medium heat 5 minutes, stirring occasionally. Garnish with sliced ripe olives and chopped parsley, if desired.

4 serving

°*Top sirloin steak may be substituted for lamb.*

Prep time: 10 minutes   **Cook time:** 20 minutes

Nutrients per serving:			
Calories	209 (28% fat)	Cholesterol	28.8 mg
Fat	6.6 g	Sodium	753.0 mg

BURGUNDY BEEF PASTA

LOW FAT/ LOW SALT

8 ounces linguine
1 pound top sirloin, very thinly sliced crosswise
2 cloves garlic, minced
½ teaspoon dried thyme
2 teaspoons vegetable oil
¼ pound mushrooms, sliced
1 can (14½ ounces) DEL MONTE® Original Recipe Stewed
   Tomatoes (No Salt Added)
1 can (8 ounces) DEL MONTE Tomato Sauce (No Salt
   Added)
¾ cup dry red wine

continued

ook pasta according to package directions; drain. In large skillet, cook meat, rlic and thyme in oil over medium-high heat 3 minutes. Add mushrooms; ok 1 minute. Add tomatoes, tomato sauce and wine. Cook, uncovered, over edium heat 15 minutes, stirring occasionally. Serve over pasta. Garnish with opped parsley, if desired.

4 servings

Prep time: 10 minutes   **Cook time:** 20 minutes

Helpful Hint: *Cook pasta ahead; rinse and drain. Cover and refrigerate. Just fore serving, heat in microwave or dip in boiling water.*

Nutrients per serving:

Calories	542 (23% fat)	Cholesterol	136.2 mg
Fat	13.6 g	Sodium	159.3 mg

RATATOUILLE

1 small eggplant, cut into ½-inch cubes
2 medium green peppers, diced
1 medium onion, sliced
1 clove garlic, minced
¼ cup olive oil
1 can (16 ounces) DEL MONTE® Zucchini With Italian-
    Style Tomato Sauce
1 can (14½ ounces) DEL MONTE Original Recipe Stewed
    Tomatoes
½ teaspoon salt
⅛ teaspoon pepper

Cook eggplant, green peppers, onion and garlic in oil over medium-high heat, stirring constantly. Add zucchini, tomatoes, salt and pepper. Cover and simmer 30 minutes. Serve with grated Parmesan cheese, if desired.

6 to 8 servings

Microwave Directions: Reduce oil to 2 tablespoons and add 2 tablespoons water. In 3-quart microwavable casserole, combine eggplant, onion, garlic, oil and water. Cover and microwave on HIGH 10 minutes, stirring halfway through. Add green pepper, zucchini, tomatoes, salt and pepper. Microwave 10 to 12 minutes, stirring halfway through.

Prep time: 15 minutes   **Cook time:** 40 minutes
Microwave cook time: 22 minutes

FISH FRANÇOISE

1 can (14½ ounces) DEL MONTE® Original Recipe Stewed
   Tomatoes
1 tablespoon lemon juice
2 cloves garlic, minced
½ teaspoon dried tarragon, crushed
⅛ teaspoon pepper
3 tablespoons whipping cream
   Vegetable oil
1½ pounds firm white fish (such as halibut or cod)
   Lemon wedges

Preheat broiler; position rack 4 inches from heat. In large saucepan, combine
tomatoes, lemon juice, garlic, tarragon and pepper. Cook, uncovered, over
medium-high heat about 10 minutes or until liquid has evaporated. Add
cream. Cook over low heat 5 minutes or until very thick; set aside. Brush
broiler pan with oil. Arrange fish on pan; season with salt and pepper, if
desired. Broil fish 3 to 4 minutes per side or until fish flakes easily with fork.
Spread tomato mixture over top of fish. Broil 1 minute. Serve immediately
with lemon wedges. *4 servings*

Prep time: 5 minutes   **Cook time**: 19 minutes

Nutrients per serving:			
Calories	240 (25% fat)	Cholesterol	77.8 m
Fat	6.6 g	Sodium	340.5 m

QUICK CASSOULET

2 slices bacon, cut into ½-inch pieces
¾ pound boneless pork chops, sliced crosswise ¼ inch thick
1 medium onion, chopped
1 clove garlic, minced
1 teaspoon dried thyme, crushed
1 can (14½ ounces) DEL MONTE® Original Recipe Stewed
   Tomatoes
½ cup dry white wine
1 can (15 ounces) white or pinto beans, drained

In large skillet, cook bacon over medium-high heat until almost crisp. Stir in
meat, onion, garlic and thyme. Season with salt and pepper, if desired. Cook
4 minutes. Add tomatoes and wine; bring to boil. Cook, uncovered, over
medium-high heat 10 minutes or until thickened, adding beans during last
5 minutes. *4 servings*

Prep & Cook time: 30 minutes

Fish Françoise

FRENCH BEEF STEW

1½ pounds stew beef, cut into 1-inch cubes
¼ cup all-purpose flour
2 tablespoons vegetable oil
2 cans (14½ ounces *each*) DEL MONTE® Original Recipe
  Stewed Tomatoes
1 can (14 ounces) beef broth
4 medium carrots, pared, cut into 1-inch chunks
2 medium potatoes, pared, cut into 1-inch chunks
¾ teaspoon dried thyme
2 tablespoons Dijon mustard (optional)

Combine meat and flour in plastic bag; toss to coat evenly. In 6-quart saucepan, brown meat in oil. Season with salt and pepper, if desired. Add remaining ingredients, except mustard. Bring to boil; reduce heat. Cover and simmer 1 hour or until beef is tender. Blend in mustard. Garnish with chopped parsley and serve with warm crusty French bread, if desired.

6 to 8 serving

Prep time: 10 minutes   **Cook time:** 1 hour

Nutrients per serving:			
Calories	281 (30% fat)	Cholesterol	61.7 m
Fat	9.3 g	Sodium	823.0 m

CHICKEN PROVENÇAL

3 tablespoons low fat plain yogurt
2 tablespoons mayonnaise
½ small clove garlic, minced
1 (3-pound) broiler-fryer chicken, cut up and skinned
½ teaspoon dried thyme
1 tablespoon vegetable oil
1 can (14½ ounces) DEL MONTE® Original Recipe Stewed
  Tomatoes
1 can (8 ounces) DEL MONTE Tomato Sauce
2 small zucchini, sliced

In small bowl, combine yogurt, mayonnaise and garlic; set aside. Sprinkle chicken with thyme. Season with salt and pepper, if desired. In large skillet, brown chicken in oil over medium-high heat; drain. Add tomatoes and tomato sauce; cover and simmer about 20 minutes or until chicken is no longer pink, stirring occasionally. Add zucchini during last 5 minutes. Serve with garlic sauce.

4 to 6 servings

Prep time: 5 minutes   **Cook time:** 30 minutes

French Beef Stew

Mexican Meals

*Savor the tastes of Mexico
with these extraordinary
south-of-the-border
meals.*

TACOS PICADILLOS

¾ pound ground pork
1 medium onion, chopped
½ teaspoon ground cinnamon
½ teaspoon ground cumin
1 can (14½ ounces) DEL MONTE® Mexican Recipe Stewed
    Tomatoes
⅛ cup DEL MONTE Seedless Raisins
⅛ cup toasted chopped almonds
6 flour tortillas

In large skillet, brown meat with onion and spices over medium-high heat.
Season to taste with salt and pepper, if desired. Stir in tomatoes and raisins.
Cover and cook 10 minutes. Remove cover; cook over medium-high heat 5
minutes or until thickened, stirring occasionally. Just before serving, stir in
almonds. Fill tortillas with meat mixture; roll to enclose. Garnish with lettuce,
cilantro and sour cream, if desired. Serve immediately.   *6 serving*

Prep time: 5 minutes   **Cook time:** 25 minutes

Helpful Hint: *If ground pork is not available, boneless pork may be
purchased and ground in food processor. Cut pork into 1-inch cubes before
processing.*

Tacos Picadillos

GRILLED PRAWNS WITH
SALSA VERA CRUZ

1 can (14½ ounces) DEL MONTE® Mexican Recipe Stewed
   Tomatoes
1 orange, peeled and chopped
¼ cup sliced green onions
¼ cup chopped cilantro or parsley
1 tablespoon olive oil
1 to 2 teaspoons minced jalapeño chile
1 small clove garlic, crushed
1 pound medium shrimp, peeled and deveined

Drain tomatoes reserving liquid; chop tomatoes. In medium bowl, combine
tomatoes, reserved liquid, orange, green onions, cilantro, oil, jalapeño and
garlic. Season to taste with salt and pepper, if desired. Thread shrimp on
skewers; season with salt and pepper, if desired. Brush grill with oil. Cook
shrimp over hot coals about 3 minutes per side or until shrimp just turn
opaque pink. Top with salsa. Serve over rice, if desired.   *4 servings*

Prep time: 27 minutes   **Cook time:** 6 minutes

Nutrients per serving:			
Calories	166 (24% fat)	Cholesterol	166.1 m
Fat	4.5 g	Sodium	463.2 m

Helpful Hint: *Thoroughly rinse shrimp in cold water before cooking.*

Grilled Prawns with Salsa Vera Cruz

SPICY QUICK AND EASY CHILI

1 pound ground beef
1 large clove garlic, minced
1 can (17 ounces) DEL MONTE® Whole Kernel Golden
    Sweet Corn, drained
1 can (16 ounces) kidney beans, drained
1 can (14½ ounces) DEL MONTE Chili Style Chunky
    Tomatoes
1 can (4 ounces) diced green chiles

In large saucepan, brown meat with garlic; drain. Add remaining ingredients.
Simmer, uncovered, 10 minutes, stirring occasionally. Garnish with green
onions, if desired.   *4 servings (1½ cups each)*

Prep & Cook time: 15 minutes

Variation: *For a zestier chili serve with hot pepper sauce or cayenne pepper.*

KIDS   Easy recipe for kids and parents to make together.

TOMATO SALSA PRONTO

1 can (14½ ounces) DEL MONTE® Mexican Recipe Stewed
    Tomatoes
¼ cup finely chopped onion
2 tablespoons chopped cilantro
2 teaspoons lemon juice
1 small clove garlic, minced
⅛ teaspoon hot pepper sauce°
    Tortilla chips

Drain tomatoes reserving liquid; pour liquid into medium bowl. Chop
tomatoes. Add tomatoes to reserved liquid. Stir in remaining ingredients,
except tortilla chips. Add additional pepper sauce, if desired. Serve with
tortilla chips.   *2 cups*

°*Substitute minced jalapeño chile to taste for hot pepper sauce.*

Prep time: 10 minutes

Helpful Hint: *Serve with meats, fish and poultry or traditional Mexican
dishes, such as tacos, burritos and quesadillas.*

Spicy Quick and Easy Chili

PIZZA SONORA

½ pound ground beef
½ teaspoon ground cumin
4 (6-inch) prepared, pre-baked pizza crusts*
1 can (14½ ounces) DEL MONTE® Pizza Style Chunky
   Tomatoes
2 cups shredded Monterey Jack cheese
1 small green pepper, thinly sliced
½ medium onion, finely chopped (optional)
1 can (4 ounces) diced green chiles

Preheat oven to 450°F. In large skillet, brown meat with cumin; drain. Place crusts on baking sheet. Spread tomatoes evenly over crusts. Top with meat mixture, ½ of cheese, pepper, onion, chiles and remaining cheese. Bake 6 to 8 minutes or until hot and bubbly.   *4 servings*

Refrigerated or frozen pizza dough may also be used; prepare and bake according to package directions.

Prep & Cook time: 25 minutes

KIDS   Easy recipe for kids and parents to make together.

FIESTA QUESO DIP

1 can (14½ ounces) DEL MONTE® Mexican Recipe Stewed
   Tomatoes
1 pound jalapeño processed cheese, diced
¼ cup sliced green onions
   Tortilla chips

In medium saucepan, combine undrained tomatoes, cheese and green onions. Cook over low heat about 12 minutes or until cheese melts, stirring frequently and breaking up tomatoes. Serve hot with chips.   *3½ cups*

Prep time: 3 minutes   **Cook time:** 12 minutes

KIDS   Easy recipe for kids and parents to make together.

Pizza Sonora

ARROZ CON POLLO

1 (3-pound) broiler-fryer chicken, cut up
½ teaspoon ground cumin
1 tablespoon vegetable oil
1 can (14½ ounces) DEL MONTE® Mexican Recipe Stewed
    Tomatoes
1 cup uncooked long grain white rice
1 can (14 ounces) chicken broth
1 large onion, thinly sliced
2 cloves garlic, minced
1 to 1½ teaspoons minced jalapeño chile

Sprinkle chicken with cumin. Season with salt and pepper, if desired. In
4-quart heavy saucepan, brown chicken in oil over medium-high heat; drain.
Drain tomatoes reserving ⅓ cup liquid. Add reserved liquid, tomatoes and
remaining ingredients to saucepan. Cover and cook over low heat about 30
minutes or until chicken is no longer pink and rice is tender.   *6 servin*

Prep & Cook time: 45 minutes

ACAPULCO EGGS

3 corn tortillas, cut into 2-inch strips
3 tablespoons butter or margarine
½ cup chopped onion
1 can (14½ ounces) DEL MONTE® Mexican Recipe Stewed
    Tomatoes
1 cup cooked ham, cut into thin strips or shredded turkey
½ cup green pepper strips
6 eggs, beaten
¾ cup shredded Monterey Jack cheese

In large skillet, cook tortilla strips in butter until golden. Remove and set
aside. Cook onion in same skillet until tender. Drain tomatoes reserving
liquid. Add reserved liquid to skillet; cook over high heat 3 minutes, stirring
frequently. Stir in tomatoes, meat and green pepper; heat through. Reduce
heat to low; add tortillas and eggs. Cover and cook 4 to 6 minutes or until egg
are set. Sprinkle with cheese; cover and cook 1 minute or until cheese is
melted. Garnish with chopped cilantro or parsley, if desired.

4 to 6 servin

Prep time: 10 minutes   **Cook time:** 15 minutes

Arroz con Poll

TORTILLA CHICKEN BAKE

1 can (14½ ounces) DEL MONTE® Mexican Recipe Stewed
 Tomatoes
½ cup chopped onion
2 cloves garlic, crushed
½ teaspoon dried oregano, crushed
½ teaspoon chili powder
½ pound boneless chicken, skinned and cut into strips
4 cups tortilla chips
¾ cup shredded jalapeño Jack cheese or Cheddar cheese

Preheat oven to 375°F. Drain tomatoes reserving liquid; chop tomatoes. In
large skillet, combine reserved liquid, onion, garlic, oregano and chili powde
boil 5 minutes, stirring occasionally. Stir in tomatoes and chicken; cook over
medium heat until chicken is no longer pink, about 3 minutes. In shallow
2-quart baking dish, layer half of chips, chicken mixture and cheese; repeat
layers ending with cheese. Cover and bake 15 minutes or until heated
through. Serve with sour cream, if desired.   *4 servin*

Prep time: 3 minutes   **Cook time:** 25 minutes

KIDS   Easy recipe for kids and parents to make together.

FESTIVE SKILLET FAJITAS   LOW FAT

1½ pounds boneless, skinless chicken, cut into ½-inch strips
1 medium onion, cut into thin wedges
2 cloves garlic, minced
1 tablespoon vegetable oil
½ teaspoon ground cumin
1 can (14½ ounces) DEL MONTE® Mexican Recipe Stewed
 Tomatoes
1 can (7 ounces) whole green chiles, drained and cut into
 strips
8 flour tortillas, warmed

continue

large skillet, brown chicken with onion and garlic in oil over medium-high
t. Stir in cumin, tomatoes and chiles; heat through. Fill warmed tortillas
h chicken mixture. Garnish with sour cream, avocado or guacamole,
ntro and lime wedges, if desired. Serve immediately.   *6 to 8 servings*

ep time: 10 minutes   **Cook time:** 10 minutes

trients per serving:

| ories | 265 (19% fat) | Cholesterol | 56.0 mg |
| | 5.5 g | Sodium | 233.0 mg |

ASY CHILI CON CARNE   LOW FAT

medium onion, chopped
stalk celery, sliced
teaspoon chili powder
can (15¼ ounces) kidney beans, drained
can (14½ ounces) **DEL MONTE® Chili Style Chunky
   Tomatoes**
cup cubed cooked beef

icrowave Directions: In 2-quart microwavable dish, combine onion,
ery and chili powder. Add 1 tablespoon water. Cover and microwave on
GH 3 to 4 minutes. Add remaining ingredients. Cover and microwave on
GH 6 to 8 minutes or until heated through, stirring halfway through. For a
icier chili, serve with hot pepper sauce.   *4 servings*

ep time: 8 minutes   **Microwave cook time:** 12 minutes

trients per serving:

| lories | 193 (16% fat) | Cholesterol | 27.5 mg |
| t | 3.4 g | Sodium | 612.0 mg |

IDS   Easy recipe for kids and parents to make together.

TURKEY ENCHILADA PIE

¾ pound ground turkey
2 teaspoons vegetable oil
1 can (14½ ounces) DEL MONTE® Mexican Recipe Stewed
    Tomatoes
1 package (1¼ ounces) taco seasoning mix
½ cup sliced green onions
1 can (2¼ ounces) sliced ripe olives, drained
6 corn tortillas
1½ cups shredded sharp Cheddar cheese

In large skillet, brown meat in oil over medium-high heat. Stir in tomatoes
and taco seasoning mix. Reduce heat; cover and cook 10 minutes, stirring
occasionally. Stir in green onions and olives. In 2-quart baking dish, place
1 tortilla in bottom; cover with about ½ cup meat sauce. Top with about
¼ cup cheese. Repeat, making a six-layer stack. Pour ½ cup water down edge
into bottom of dish. Cover with foil and bake at 425°F, 30 minutes or until
heated through. Cut into 4 wedges. Garnish with sour cream, if desired.

4 servin

Prep time: 15 minutes   **Cook time:** 48 minutes

ARROZ MEXICANA   LOW FA

1 medium onion, chopped
2 cloves garlic, crushed
⅛ teaspoon dried oregano, crushed
1 tablespoon vegetable oil
¾ cup uncooked long grain white rice
1 can (14½ ounces) DEL MONTE® Mexican Recipe Stewed
    Tomatoes
1 green pepper, chopped

In large skillet, cook onion, garlic and oregano in oil until onion is tender. Sti
in rice; cook until rice is golden, stirring frequently. Drain tomatoes reserving
liquid; pour liquid into measuring cup. Add water to measure 1½ cups. Stir
into rice; bring to boil. Reduce heat; cover and simmer over medium heat
15 minutes or until rice is tender. Stir in tomatoes and green pepper; cook
5 minutes. Garnish with chopped parsley, if desired.   *4 to 6 servin*

Prep time: 5 minutes   **Cook time:** 27 minutes

Nutrients per serving:			
Calories	166 (17% fat)	Cholesterol	0.0 m
Fat	3.1 g	Sodium	211.6 m

Turkey Enchilada P

American Favorites

Travel across America in a culinary adventure that includes both coasts, the heartland, the deep south and the desert southwest.

ROSEMARY CHICKEN SAUTÉ PIZZA

2 half boneless chicken breasts, skinned and cut into strips
1 medium onion, sliced
½ teaspoon dried rosemary, crushed
1 tablespoon vegetable oil
1 (12-inch) prepared, pre-baked pizza crust°
1 can (14½ ounces) DEL MONTE® Pizza Style Chunky Tomatoes
2 cups shredded mozzarella cheese
1 green, yellow or red pepper, sliced

Preheat oven to 450°F. In large skillet, cook chicken, onion and rosemary in oil over medium-high heat; drain. Place crust on baking sheet. Spread tomatoes evenly over crust. Top with ½ of cheese, then chicken mixture, pepper slices and remaining cheese. Bake 10 minutes or until hot and bubbl'

4 to 6 servin

°*Substitute 4 (6-inch) prepared, pre-baked pizza crusts. Refrigerated or froze pizza dough may also be used; prepare and bake according to package directions.*

Prep time: 10 minutes   **Cook time:** 10 minutes

Rosemary Chicken Sauté Pizz

ARIZONA PORK CHILI

1½ pounds boneless pork, cut into ¼-inch cubes
 1 tablespoon vegetable oil
 1 onion, coarsely chopped
 2 cloves garlic, minced
 1 can (15 ounces) black, pinto or kidney beans, drained
 1 can (14½ ounces) DEL MONTE® Chili Style Chunky
    Tomatoes
 1 can (4 ounces) diced green chiles
 1 teaspoon ground cumin

In large skillet, brown meat in oil over medium-high heat. Add onion and garlic; cook until onion is tender. Season with salt and pepper, if desired. Add remaining ingredients. Simmer 10 minutes, stirring occasionally. Serve with tortillas and sour cream, if desired.   *6 servin*

Prep time: 10 minutes   **Cook time:** 25 minutes

CHEESEBURGER MACARONI

1 pound ground beef
 1 cup chopped onion
 1 can (14½ ounces) DEL MONTE® Original Recipe Stewed
    Tomatoes
 1 cup elbow macaroni
1½ cups shredded Longhorn or sharp Cheddar cheese

In large skillet, brown meat and onion over medium-high heat; drain. Season with salt and pepper, if desired. Add 1 cup water and tomatoes; bring to boil. Stir in macaroni. Cover and simmer 10 minutes or until macaroni is tender. Stir in cheese. Garnish with sour cream, if desired.   *5 to 6 servin*

Prep time: 5 minutes   **Cook time:** 20 minutes

KIDS   Easy recipe for kids and parents to make together.

Arizona Pork Chil

TOMATO SCALLOPED POTATOES

1 can (14½ ounces) DEL MONTE® Original Recipe Stewed
    Tomatoes
1 pound red potatoes, thinly sliced
1 medium onion, chopped
½ cup whipping cream
1 cup shredded Swiss cheese
3 tablespoons grated Parmesan cheese

Preheat oven to 350°F. Drain tomatoes reserving liquid; pour liquid into
measuring cup. Add water to measure 1 cup. In large skillet, add reserved
liquid, potatoes and onion; cover and cook over medium-high heat 10 minut
or until tender. Place in 1-quart baking dish and top with tomatoes and
cream. Sprinkle with cheeses. Bake 20 minutes or until hot and bubbly.
Sprinkle with chopped parsley, if desired.   *6 servin*

Prep time: 8 minutes   **Cook time:** 30 minutes

CHILI BEAN DEL MONTE

¾ cup sliced green onions
1 can (15 ounces) pinto beans, drained
1 can (14½ ounces) DEL MONTE® Chili Style Chunky
    Tomatoes
1 can (8¾ ounces) or 1 cup kidney beans, drained
½ to 1 teaspoon minced jalapeño chile
½ teaspoon ground cumin
¼ teaspoon garlic powder
¼ cup shredded sharp Cheddar cheese

Set aside ¼ cup green onions for garnish. In large skillet, combine remaining
½ cup green onions with remaining ingredients except cheese. Bring to boil;
reduce heat to medium. Cook 5 minutes. Serve with cheese and reserved
onions.   *3 servings (approximately ¾ cup each*

Prep & Cook time: 15 minutes

Tomato Scalloped Potatoe

SAUSAGE HAM JAMBALAYA

6 ounces spicy smoked sausage links, sliced
6 ounces cooked ham, diced
2 cans (14½ ounces *each*) DEL MONTE® Cajun Recipe
   Stewed Tomatoes
1 cup uncooked long grain white rice
1 large clove garlic, minced
1 tablespoon chopped fresh parsley
1 bay leaf

In heavy 4-quart saucepan, brown sausage and ham. Drain tomatoes reservi
liquid; pour liquid into measuring cup. Add water to measure 1½ cups. Add
reserved liquid, tomatoes and remaining ingredients to sausage mixture.
Cover and simmer 30 to 35 minutes, stirring occasionally. Remove bay leaf.
Garnish with additional chopped parsley, if desired.   *4 to 6 servin*

Prep time: 10 minutes   **Cook time:** 40 minutes

SOUTHERN BBQ CHILI   LOW FAT

½ pound lean ground beef
1 medium onion, chopped
1 clove garlic, minced
1 can (14½ ounces) DEL MONTE® Chili Style Chunky
   Tomatoes
1 can (15 ounces) barbecue-style beans
1 can (15 ounces) black beans, drained
1 can (8¾ ounces) or 1 cup kidney beans, drained

In large saucepan, brown meat, onion and garlic; drain. Add tomatoes and
beans. Cover and simmer 15 minutes or until heated through. Garnish with
low fat sour cream and sliced green onions, if desired.

6 servings (approximately 1 cup eac

Prep time: 5 minutes   **Cook time:** 20 minutes

Nutrients per serving:			
Calories	243 (20% fat)	Cholesterol	23.0 m
Fat	5.7 g	Sodium	830.0 m

KIDS   Easy recipe for kids and parents to make together.

Sausage Ham Jambalay

CREOLE MACARONI AND CHEESE

½ cup butter or margarine
1 package (12 ounces) elbow macaroni
1 can (14½ ounces) DEL MONTE® Cajun Recipe Stewed
    Tomatoes
1 teaspoon salt
½ teaspoon white pepper
1 tablespoon all-purpose flour
1 can (12 fluid ounces) evaporated milk
2 cups shredded sharp Cheddar cheese

In large skillet, melt butter. Add macaroni, tomatoes, salt and pepper. Cook
5 minutes stirring occasionally. Add 1½ cups water; bring to boil. Cover and
simmer 20 minutes or until macaroni is tender. Sprinkle in flour; blend well.
Stir in evaporated milk and cheese. Simmer 5 minutes, stirring occasionally,
until cheese is completely melted. Garnish with green pepper or parsley, if
desired. Serve immediately.   *4 to 6 servir*

Prep & Cook time: 35 minutes

KIDS Easy recipe for kids and parents to make together.

CONNECTICUT BEAN SKILLET

½ pound hot Italian sausage links, sliced
½ pound Polish sausage links, sliced
1 large onion, chopped
3 cans (16 ounces *each*) pork and beans
1 can (14½ ounces) DEL MONTE® Original Recipe Stewed
    Tomatoes
2 tablespoons Dijon mustard
1 teaspoon dried basil, crushed

In large skillet, brown sausages and onion over medium-high heat; drain. Add
remaining ingredients. Simmer 15 minutes. Serve with tossed green salad and
Boston brown bread, if desired.   *4 to 6 serving*

Prep time: 7 minutes   **Cook time:** 18 minutes

CO PIZZA

(7-inch) flour tortillas
can (16 ounces) refried beans
teaspoon ground cumin
can (14½ ounces) DEL MONTE® Pizza Style Chunky
    Tomatoes
cups shredded sharp Cheddar or Monterey Jack cheese
cups shredded lettuce
cup sour cream

heat oven to 450°F. Place tortillas on baking sheet. Spread beans evenly
r tortillas. Stir cumin into tomatoes. Spread over beans. Top with cheese.
e 6 to 8 minutes or until hot and bubbly. Serve with lettuce and sour
m.   *6 pizzas*

p time: 5 minutes   **Cook time:** 8 minutes

)s   Easy recipe for kids and parents to make together.

NTA FE CORN BAKE

pound ground beef
medium onion, chopped
clove garlic, minced
teaspoon dried oregano
cans (14½ ounces *each*) DEL MONTE® Chili Style Chunky
    Tomatoes
can (17 ounces) DEL MONTE Whole Kernel Golden
    Sweet Corn, drained
package (8½ ounces) corn muffin mix, plus ingredients to
    prepare mix

large skillet, brown meat with onion, garlic and oregano over medium-high
at; drain. Season with salt and pepper, if desired. Add tomatoes and corn.
ur into 2-quart baking dish. Prepare muffin mix according to package
ections. Spread evenly over meat mixture. Bake at 400°F, 25 to 30 minutes
until golden.   *8 servings*

ep time: 5 minutes   **Cook time:** 35 minutes

BLUE CHEESE CHICKEN SALAD

1 can (14½ ounces) DEL MONTE® Original Recipe Stewed
  Tomatoes
½ pound boneless chicken, skinned and cut into strips
½ teaspoon dried tarragon
6 cups torn assorted lettuces
½ medium red onion, thinly sliced
½ medium cucumber, thinly sliced
⅓ cup crumbled blue cheese
¼ cup Italian dressing

Drain tomatoes reserving liquid. In large skillet, cook reserved liquid until
thickened, about 5 minutes, stirring occasionally. Add chicken and tarragon
cook until chicken is no longer pink, stirring frequently. Cool. In large bowl
toss chicken and tomato liquid with remaining ingredients.   *4 servi*

Prep time: 10 minutes   **Cook time:** 10 minutes

CAJUN CLAM CHOWDER

6 slices bacon, diced
½ pound red potatoes, diced
2 medium onions, chopped
2 stalks celery, sliced
3 tablespoons all-purpose flour
1 can (10 ounces) whole baby clams
2 cans (14½ ounces *each*) DEL MONTE® Cajun Recipe
  Stewed Tomatoes
1 bottle (8 ounces) clam juice
¼ to ½ teaspoon hot pepper sauce

In Dutch oven, cook bacon until slightly crisp. Drain reserving 3 tablespoon
drippings. Add potatoes, onions and celery; cook over medium-high heat un
tender-crisp, about 10 minutes. Sprinkle with flour; cook 1 to 2 minutes.
Drain clams reserving liquid. Add reserved liquid, tomatoes, clam juice and
1 cup water to vegetables. Cook 20 to 25 minutes or until potatoes are tende
Stir in clams and hot pepper sauce; heat through.

6 servings (approximately 1 cup eac

Prep & Cook time: 45 minutes

KIDS   Easy recipe for kids and parents to make together.

Blue Cheese Chicken Sal

MANHATTAN TURKEY A LA KING

8 ounces wide egg noodles
1 pound boneless turkey or chicken, cut into strips
1 tablespoon vegetable oil
1 can (14½ ounces) DEL MONTE® Pasta Style Chunky
    Tomatoes
1 can (10¾ ounces) condensed cream of celery soup
1 medium onion, chopped
2 stalks celery, sliced
1 cup sliced mushrooms

Cook noodles according to package directions; drain. In large skillet, brow
turkey in oil over medium-high heat. Season with salt and pepper, if desire
Add remaining ingredients, except noodles. Cover and cook over medium
heat 5 minutes. Remove cover; cook 5 minutes or until thickened, stirring
occasionally. Serve over hot noodles. Garnish with chopped parsley, if desi

6 serv.

Prep time: 7 minutes   **Cook time:** 20 minutes

Helpful Hint: *Cook pasta ahead; rinse and drain. Cover and refrigerate. J*
before serving, heat in microwave or dip in boiling water.

BAYOU DIRTY RICE

¼ pound spicy sausage, crumbled
½ medium onion, chopped
1 stalk celery, sliced
1 package (6 ounces) wild and long grain rice seasoned mix
1 can (14½ ounces) DEL MONTE® Cajun Recipe Stewed
    Tomatoes
½ green pepper, chopped
¼ cup chopped parsley

In large skillet, brown sausage and onion over medium-high heat; drain.
Add celery, rice and rice seasoning packet; cook and stir 2 minutes. Drain
tomatoes reserving liquid; pour liquid into measuring cup. Add water to
measure 1⅓ cups; pour over rice. Add tomatoes; bring to boil. Cover and co
over low heat 20 minutes. Add pepper and parsley. Cover and cook 5 minut
or until rice is tender. Serve with roasted chicken or Cornish game hens.

4 to 6 servi

Prep & Cook time: 40 minutes

Manhattan Turkey à la K

CAJUN CHILI

6 ounces spicy sausage links, sliced
4 boneless chicken thighs, skinned and cut into cubes
1 medium onion, chopped
⅛ teaspoon cayenne pepper
1 can (15 ounces) black-eyed peas or kidney beans, drained
1 can (14½ ounces) DEL MONTE® Chili Style Chunky
     Tomatoes
1 medium green pepper, chopped

In large skillet, lightly brown sausage over medium-high heat. Add chicken,
onion and cayenne pepper; cook until browned. Drain. Stir in remaining
ingredients. Cook over medium-high heat 5 minutes, stirring occasionally.

4 serv

Prep & Cook time: 20 minutes

SHRIMP BISQUE

1 pound medium shrimp, peeled and deveined
½ cup chopped onion
½ cup chopped celery
½ cup chopped carrot
2 tablespoons butter or margarine
2 cans (14 ounces *each*) chicken broth
1 can (14½ ounces) DEL MONTE® Original Recipe Stewed
     Tomatoes
¼ teaspoon dried thyme
1 cup half & half

Cut shrimp into small pieces; set aside. In large saucepan, cook onion, celery
and carrot in butter until onion is tender. Add shrimp; cook 1 minute. Add
broth, tomatoes and thyme; simmer 10 minutes. Ladle ⅓ of soup into blender
container or food processor. Cover and process until smooth. Repeat for
remaining soup. Return to saucepan. Add half & half. Heat through.
Do not boil.   *6 servings (approximately 1 cup eac*

Prep time: 15 minutes   **Cook time:** 20 minutes

Variation: Substitute 2 cans (6 ounces *each*) of crab for shrimp.

Cajun Ch

HEARTLAND SHEPHERD'S PIE

¾ pound ground beef
1 medium onion, chopped
1 can (14½ ounces) DEL MONTE® Original Recipe Stewed
   Tomatoes
1 can (8 ounces) DEL MONTE Tomato Sauce
1 can (16 ounces) DEL MONTE Mixed Vegetables, drained
   Instant mashed potato flakes plus ingredients to prepare
   (enough for 6 servings)
3 cloves garlic, minced

Preheat oven to 375°F. In large skillet, brown meat and onion over medium
high heat; drain. Add tomatoes and tomato sauce; cook over high heat until
thickened, stirring frequently. Stir in mixed vegetables. Season with salt
and pepper, if desired. Spoon into 2-quart baking dish; set aside. Prepare
6 servings mashed potatoes according to package directions, first cooking
garlic in specified amount of butter. Top meat mixture with potatoes. Bake
20 minutes or until heated through. Garnish with chopped parsley,
if desired. *4 to 6 servin*

Prep time: 5 minutes   **Cook time:** 30 minutes

SLOPPY DOGS

1 can (15 ounces) pinto or kidney beans, drained
1 can (14½ ounces) DEL MONTE® Chili Style Chunky
   Tomatoes
2 fully cooked hot dogs, sliced crosswise
1 teaspoon prepared mustard
4 hamburger buns, split
½ cup shredded Cheddar cheese

Microwave Directions: In 2-quart microwavable dish, combine all
ingredients, except buns and cheese. Cover and microwave on HIGH
6 to 8 minutes or until heated through. Place buns on paper towel; microwav
on HIGH 30 seconds to 1 minute. Place buns on 4 dishes, cut side up. Spoor
chili over buns. Top with cheese. Serve immediately.   *4 serving*

Prep time: 5 minutes   **Cook time:** 9 minutes

KIDS   Easy recipe for kids and parents to make together.

Heartland Shepherd's Pi

BLACK BEAN GARNACHAS

1 can (14½ ounces) DEL MONTE® Mexican Recipe Stewed
    Tomatoes
1 can (15 ounces) black or pinto beans, drained
2 cloves garlic, minced
1 to 2 teaspoons minced jalapeño chiles (optional)
½ teaspoon ground cumin
1 cup cubed grilled chicken
4 flour tortillas
½ cup shredded sharp Cheddar cheese

Drain tomatoes reserving liquid; chop tomatoes. In large skillet, combine
tomatoes, reserved liquid, beans, garlic, jalapeño and cumin. Cook over
medium-high heat, 5 to 7 minutes or until thickened, stirring occasionally.
Season with salt and pepper, if desired. Add chicken. Arrange tortillas in a
single layer on grill over medium coals. Spread about ¾ cup chicken mixtur
over each tortilla. Top with cheese. Cook about 3 minutes or until bottom
tortilla browns and cheese melts. Garnish with shredded lettuce and diced
avocado, if desired.   *4 serv*

Prep time: 5 minutes   **Cook time:** 10 minutes

Nutrients per serving:			
Calories	372 (20% fat)	Cholesterol	45.0
Fat	8.5 g	Sodium	386.0

CAJUN CHICKEN

2½ pounds chicken pieces, skinned (breasts, thighs, legs)
1 tablespoon vegetable oil
2 cloves garlic, crushed
½ teaspoon dried thyme
1 can (14½ ounces) DEL MONTE® Cajun Recipe Stewed
    Tomatoes
1 red or green pepper, cut into strips
1 stalk celery, sliced
1 carrot, thinly sliced

In large skillet, brown chicken in oil over medium-high heat, 10 to
15 minutes; drain. Season with salt and pepper, if desired. Stir garlic and
thyme into tomatoes; pour over chicken. Add pepper strips, celery and carr
Bring to boil; cover and simmer 15 minutes or until chicken is no longer pi
Garnish with sliced green onions, if desired.   *4 to 6 servi*

Prep time: 8 minutes   **Cook time:** 30 minutes

Black Bean Garnach

LOUISIANA PORK CHOPS

1 teaspoon garlic powder
¼ teaspoon black pepper
¼ teaspoon white pepper
¼ teaspoon cayenne pepper
4 pork chops, ¾ inch thick
1 tablespoon butter or margarine
1 can (14½ ounces) DEL MONTE® Cajun Recipe Stewed
   Tomatoes

Combine garlic powder and peppers. Sprinkle on both sides of meat. In larg
skillet, heat butter over medium-high heat. Add meat; cook 5 minutes. Turr
over and cook 4 minutes; drain. Add tomatoes. Cover and cook over mediur
heat 10 minutes or until meat is cooked. Remove meat to serving dish; keep
warm. Cook sauce until thickened; spoon over meat.   *4 servir*

Prep time: 5 minutes   **Cook time:** 21 minutes

NEW ENGLAND
FISHERMAN'S SKILLET   LOW FAT/LOW SALT

4 small red potatoes, diced
1 medium onion, chopped
1 tablespoon olive oil
2 stalks celery, chopped
2 cloves garlic, minced
⅛ teaspoon dried thyme, crushed
1 can (14½ ounces) DEL MONTE® Original Recipe Stewed
   Tomatoes (No Salt Added)
1 pound firm white fish (such as halibut, snapper or cod)

In large skillet, brown potatoes and onion in oil over medium-high heat,
stirring occasionally. Season with salt-free herb seasoning mix, if desired. Stir
in celery, garlic and thyme; cook 4 minutes. Add tomatoes; bring to boil. Coo
4 minutes or until thickened. Add fish; cover and cook over medium heat 5 t
8 minutes or until fish flakes easily with fork. Garnish with lemon wedges an
chopped parsley, if desired.   *4 serving*

Prep time: 10 minutes   **Cook time:** 25 minutes

Nutrients per serving:			
Calories	214 (22% fat)	Cholesterol	42.0 m
Fat	5.2 g	Sodium	132.0 m

92   AMERICAN FAVORITES

Index

METRIC CONVERSION CHART

VOLUME MEASUREMENT (dry)

⅛ teaspoon = .5 mL
¼ teaspoon = 1 mL
½ teaspoon = 2 mL
¾ teaspoon = 4 mL
1 teaspoon = 5 mL
1 tablespoon = 15 mL
2 tablespoons = 25 mL
¼ cup = 50 mL
⅓ cup = 75 mL
⅔ cup = 150 mL
¾ cup = 175 mL
1 cup = 250 mL
2 cups = 1 pint = 500 mL
3 cups = 750 mL
4 cups = 1 quart = 1 L

VOLUME MEASUREMENT (fluid)

1 fluid ounce (2 tablespoons) = 30 mL
4 fluid ounces (½ cup) = 125 mL
8 fluid ounces (1 cup) = 250 mL
12 fluid ounces (1½ cups) = 375 mL
16 fluid ounces (2 cups) = 500 mL

WEIGHT (MASS)

½ ounce = 15 g
1 ounce = 30 g
3 ounces = 85 g
3.75 ounces = 100 g
4 ounces = 115 g
8 ounces = 225 g
12 ounces = 340 g
16 ounces = 1 pound = 450 g

DIMENSION

$\frac{1}{16}$ inch = 2 mm
⅛ inch = 3 mm
¼ inch = 6 mm
½ inch = 1.5 cm
¾ inch = 2 cm
1 inch = 2.5 cm

OVEN TEMPERATURE

250°F = 120°C
275°F = 140°C
300°F = 150°C
325°F = 160°C
350°F = 180°C
375°F = 190°C
400°F = 200°C
425°F = 220°C
450°F = 230°C

BAKING PAN SIZES

Utensil	Inches/ Quarts	Metric Volume	Centimeter
Baking or	8 × 8 × 2	2 L	20 × 20
Cake pan	9 × 9 × 2	2.5 L	22 × 22
(square or	12 × 8 × 2	3 L	30 × 20
rectangular)	13 × 9 × 2	3.5 L	33 × 23
Loaf Pan	8 × 4 × 3	1.5 L	20 × 10
	9 × 5 × 3	2 L	23 × 13
Round Layer	8 × 1½	1.2 L	20 × 4
Cake Pan	9 × 1½	1.5 L	23 × 4
Pie Plate	8 × 1¼	750 mL	20 × 3
	9 × 1¼	1 L	23 × 3
Baking Dish	1 quart	1 L	
or	1½ quart	1.5 L	
Casserole	2 quart	2 L	